— *When The Ligh*

"This fun, inspiring book on life is one I would most definitely
recommend to everyone who enjoys Self-Help books & poetry. Phyllis
Zuccarello shares her life lessons with common sense & touching
poems. This book is one everyone can read and take something out
of & apply to their own lives. This book can help you through tough
times, make you laugh & touch your heart. It also helps us realize that
no matter what our situation, we are all in this life together! Read it
& pass it along to all the folks you care about! My mom read Phylliss'
book also & just fell in love with it. Definitely a GREAT read!"

—Jennifer Proctor

"This is a great book that is very hard to put down! I read it from
start to finish and pulled a lot from the wisdom on its pages. Phyllis
Zuccarello is very talented and has a way of putting serious issues
into a style of writing anyone can enjoy. I have recommended this
book to friends and family and will continue to tell others about it."

—Steven Zink

"It's so easy to get swept away in the busy-ness of life and to forget
about what makes life rich and wonderful and worth living. Just
take the time to read *"When The Lights Are On But Nobody's Home"*
and you will instantly be re-focused on the important and significant
things in life. Don't miss out - I promise these simple nuggets of
wisdom sprinkled with honesty and humility will put you back on
track. The author wonderfully communicates many awe-inspiring
truths in a way that will impact any reader. Just be sure after you
read it to pass it along. If everyone read this book the world would
be a much better place. I know I am a better person."

—Dale Kloefkorn

"It is very evident that the author Phyllis Zuccarello is a very
gifted and talented woman. I am amazed the way she packs such
trememdous words of wisdom in each page. You can't keep yourself
from loving and admiring her when you see how she has poured out
her heart through her writings. This book was very touching to me
and I know I will refer to it and share it with many others."

—Priscilla A. Monahan

When the Lights Are On But Nobody's Home

*A Book That Brings Reality Back
To Make You Think…Again.*

Revised Edition 2012

Available at Amazon.com

When the Lights Are On But Nobody's Home
A Book That Brings Reality Back
To Make You Think…Again.

ISBN 978-1470039721

Book layout: www.markgelotte.com

Wise are those who live each day to look back with no regrets.

To My Children: Kendra, Dylan, Joel and Lindsey.

My Grandchildren: Alex, Scott, David, Kara, River,
Kylee, Kailee, P.J., Aidan, Isaiah, Emma, Chloe,
Alyssa and Kadynce.

Maggy Colby, who I admire most for her ability
to keep going…no matter what.

Bill Colby, for his patience and support.
Sam, for helping me with the cover.
Sally Brown, for her huge amount
of encouragement.

And to all who appreciate life,
by making it matter.

CONTENTS

CONTENTS

CONTENTS

It's About Time

The time goes by so fast.

Before we know, it's the past

And our days are spent

Thinking where the years went.

What was once far away

Seems just like it was yesterday.

We feel our regrets and then,

Wish we could do it over again.

So take time along the way

To realize what matters today.

Make the difference now, don't wait

Before you know… it's too late.

The Importance of Realizing What Matters

The most beneficial thought process "I believe" we go through
in life, is coming to a realization. We can accomplish so much
by putting this into action and seeing it all the way through.
Leaving no loose ends to look back at and wonder about.

In today's society however, we seem to be so caught up in one thing
or another...we often lose sight of what we should be paying
more attention to. As the old saying goes, "We can't see the forest
for the trees." Consequently, by the time we realize what that is...
It's too late.

As you turn the pages of this book, you will have the chance
to reflect on life's many realities, "without the trees," so to speak.
Each one is based on the facts of its matter and gets right to
the point. You won't have to read in between the lines

Take this time to identify with feelings you may have, but
perhaps you can't find the right words to put them into.
Learn what it takes to have a fulfilling relationship, as well
as to build character and self-esteem, and...discover
all the right reasons for having appreciation.

This book was written to make you think...again. I am in
hopes that you allow these original writings to help you
realize what matters in your life, so you can look back
with no regrets, and remember: the way you live
not only affects you, but those you love.

TRULY, A POETIC EXPERIENCE

PART ONE

Becoming Wise to Know the Difference

Face Reality, My Friend

As you are taking this journey
Words of wisdom come your way:

Pay attention to what they have to say.

On every road you will learn something new.
So be sure you take them all the way through.

You will find reasons to make time for things.
As well as how to deal with what life brings.

And when this journey is over, you will surely know
How to make life matter wherever you go.

Now it's all about reality from beginning to end,
And if you want to become wise…

It's best to face this first, my friend!

Why Worry?

It takes joy away from life by worrying what's ahead.
Life's too short to worry and you'll be miserable instead.

What's going to happen will happen, so why get stressed?
In the end you just may find things turned out for the best.

Keep a positive outlook and make the most of each day.
When something comes up…get on it right away.

It's a waste of time to worry, it wears a mind out.
And … if you're doing what you should,

Then what's there to worry about?

Moods, Moods, and More Moods

A good mood spreads joy.
A bad one tends to annoy.
A strange one brings on a stare.
A blah one needs a repair.
A great one shows off your best.
A frustrated one stresses the rest.
A rare one can help you grow.
A passive one won't let you say no.
A terrible one brings down the house.
An ugly one can make you a louse.
A terrific one goes a long way.
A weird one can mess up your day.
An energetic one makes you try.
A sad one can cause you to cry.
A curious one can help you learn.
A serious one makes you seem stern.
A lousy one can make the day drag.
A generous one shouldn't have a price tag.
A sentimental one brings back the past.
A romantic one makes the night last.
A talkative one can bend an ear.
A lackadaisical one makes things unclear.
A positive one will make your day.
A nagging one keeps others away.
A crazy one can help you explore.
A dull one can make you a bore.
A joking one can hurt a heart.
A negative one has a bad start.

A rotten one will begin to stink.
A melancholy one makes you think.
A stupid one can cause you to fall.
A magnificent one is the best of them all.

You can be in a mood and not know why.
Perhaps you can't shake it, no matter how you try.
It could stay with you for days, or…go away fast.
You may even enjoy it and hope for it to last.

However, should one become nasty
And you want to keep friends?
It's best to hide behind closed doors
Until that mood ends.

Say What You Mean, and Mean What You Say

NEVER SAY NEVER:

You never know if you are going to change your mind.
Yet, if you say you will, and don't: respect you will never find.

Never say you're sorry when you're not; words alone won't get it.
Yet, if you hold back when you are: you will only end up regretting it.

It's important in life to be the person that you are!
But say what you mean, and mean what you say

Or in life, you will never get far.

Read the Writing on the Wall

Before judging others, look at your ways.
Look at your past…then judge your own days.

Before criticizing others, think of what this can do.
It can put them on the defensive, to come back on you.

And before holding a grudge, you should try letting it go.
We all make mistakes, including yourself, you know.

Remember: no one is perfect…not you, nor me.
And things aren't always what they appear to be.

Now take a long hard look at the writing on the wall:
"If you can't find something nice to say,

Don't say anything at all."

Use Tact, for Goodness' Sake

If you have to say what could hurt a friend:
Choose your words from beginning to end.

For them to understand, you must use tact.
The way you say it is how they will react.

Considering their feelings will clearly show…
What you're telling them is important they know.

And they will listen.

Avoid that Gossip

Confiding in another may be something to regret.
If you think it won't…think again yet.

When you open up to someone you expect it to stay there,
But don't be surprised if they pass it on somewhere.

It'll get blown out of proportion, turned it inside-out.
And become gossip for others to spread about.

What it boils down to is to be careful what you say.
If you are careful who you tell what to:

It will keep the gossip away.

Don't Ignore Your Problems

Facing problems can be tough.
You may think you had enough.
But don't ignore them…if you do,
They'll only end up following you.

Now they're big instead of small.
You're overwhelmed by them all.
Wishing you would have done then
What you have to try to… again.

Why not look at each one as a test.
And when it's over, put it to rest.
It's the only way to be strong
For others that come along.

Otherwise, life will suck for you.
And I'm sure you don't want it to.
So take this piece of advice today:
When problems come up…

Face them right away.

When You Give Freely

There are people who give expecting something back.
Their character is weak. Compassion they lack.

Others give freely and have character that is fine.
It's coming from the heart. With kindness, they shine.

Those who don't give at all are selfish in their ways.
They will never understand how giving often pays.

You see, giving freely… especially to someone in need
Makes you feel so good inside. Oh yes…indeed.

As Far As the Conscience Goes!

Going by your conscience is the only way to go.
Otherwise, my friend, this is how you know:

You hurt by your actions and you may not heal
When you think doing wrong is no big deal.

Saying it's OK to do something that is not,
Can make you lose…everything you've got.

You can't escape from it, there is no way.
Sooner or later you face it, and…you pay.

So it's wise to let it be your guide.
Because from your conscience…

You cannot hide.

Hold On To Your Identity

To avoid getting trapped

And becoming "one of a bunch:"

THINK…

Before rolling with a punch.

Friends will try and take you

Wherever they are going,

And can get you there

Without you even knowing.

Hold on to your identity,

And be careful what you do.

Staying out of trouble…

Depends on you!

To All Single Parents

Being a single parent is something to learn.
When dealing with kids, you got to be stern.
Otherwise they think they can run the show,
And never understand the meaning of "no."

As far as the bills, you can't let them wait.
Or count on child support "not to be late."
Stay on a budget and tuck money away.
As the old saying goes: "for a rainy day."

And it's always important to take time for you.
Or you'll just be doing "what you got to do."
Then stress will get you in one way or another.
You may even regret being a father or a mother.

So to all single parents out there:
It may be tough, but don't think it's unfair.
Kids will feel they're a burden if you do.
Making it hard for a family to get through.

Why Take Chances?

If you want to take a chance

But don't know…you should:

I say, "why not?"

It can be something good.

Ah, but what if it isn't?

Well look at it like this:

It is an opportunity

You don't want to miss.

You learn from experience

What you can't from any book.

And this makes it all worth

Taking a chance you took.

Some Things You Just Can't Change

You can't stop the rain from falling
Or the sky from turning gray.
Mother Nature is the only one
Calling shots along the way.

You can't return to the past
And take back what's already gone.
You can only learn from it,
And continue to move on.

You can't expect someone to be
The way you think they should.
You can only set an example,
And in time hope they would.

You can't take things for granted
When they could change so fast.
You can only make the best of them
…while they last.

No, you can't change something
That's impossible to,
But you should…those you can
If you know they are hurting you.

Taking a Break

It's hard to do what's right in a world of unpredictable turns.
So I dance the dance all night while frustration slowly burns.

It's not easy to face reality in a life filled with uncertainty.
I try my best, but sometimes…things get the best of me.

I dance the dance to take a break from what life deals.
I get tired, but can't sleep…feeling good by the way it all feels.

Come dance with me, my friend, to the tune of feeling free.
It's always better to take a break…than to give up on reality.

Teach Them While They Are Young

Kids become problems when you don't teach them young,
How to mind their manners, and how to control their tongue.

If you fail to put your foot down, they will walk all over you.
And show you no respect...no matter what you try to do.

They need your guidance, so be sure to let them know
You're the captain of the ship and respect they must show.

Don't let them become problems. Life is hard enough.
Remember who is in charge, and if need be...get tough.

They will always look up to you with the respect shown.
And because you taught them...while they were young:

They take pride in the way they have grown.

It's Time to Break that Habit

Don't gamble if you can't afford to lose.
You'll only go home crying the blues.
Oh, you may win every now and then.
Just to end up losing it again.

Casino's can really suck you in.
You play and play thinking you'll win.
Sometimes you're there night and day.
Until you gamble all your money away.

Even if you buy a scratcher or two,
The odds are always against you.
As for betting on horses, it can be fun,
But won't be…unless you've won.

Gambling is a hard habit to break.
Think before you do, for goodness sake.
Be wise with your money, it's no joke.
No one wants to go through life…broke.

Keep an Eye Out For Ruts

On life's roads there are many, many ruts.
Falling into one will surely drive you nuts.

Retrace your steps so you know how you fell.
Being in a rut, could become a living hell.

Your thinking is negative. Nothing goes right.
If you don't try to look up, you barely see light.

Self-pity takes over. You think only of regrets.
And the longer this goes on…the deeper it gets.

So when you see one coming, find a different route.
Once you're in a rut … it's hard to get out.

Could This Be Menopause?

You're going crazy…people drive you up a wall.

You worry about things that you shouldn't…at all.

You get bored easy, you're always uptight.

You're unable to sleep, you toss and turn all night.

You keep losing things. You think it's in your mind.

Wherever you go you leave something behind.

One minute you're happy. The next…you cry.

You're unable to cope, and you don't know why.

Now if this is about you, I would venture to say:

"Get those hormones checked, and do it right away."

How to Feel Your Best

If you want to feel good: this is what you do.
Stay away from things that are bad for you.
Eat less meat, cut out the white bread.
Try more fruits and veggies instead.

Drink a lot of liquids, less soda pop.
If you smoke cigarettes…it's time to stop.
Think before you eat any processed foods.
MSG will only mess with your moods.

If you like coffee, try caffeine free.
It won't make you feel so jittery.
It's good to take vitamins of every kind:
You'll think with a much clearer mind.

And don't eat things that'll put on weight.
Always eat early, never when it's late.
Limit the amount of alcohol you drink.
It'll surely screw up the way you think.

Now perhaps you'd like to go down a size.
Well, it wouldn't hurt for you to exercise.
And for goodness' sake, don't stress out.
It'll age you quicker, without a doubt.

But if you really want to feel your best:
Always, always… get plenty of rest.

Forgiving…A Must

Healing comes with time, as the memories slowly fade.

With time, perhaps you realize mistakes that were made.

Though pain lessens and tears stop, anger will go on.

Though yesterday is the past, the memories are never gone.

Yes! Time heals, leaving scars to remind you along the way

That unless you are forgiving…especially of yourself:

You won't have a peaceful day.

It's Time to Move On

Memories may take over. You think you can't go on.

Memories of what you had: of a life, that is now gone.

It's time to accept the facts. It's time to move on and grow.

Even if you had it back… it wouldn't be the same, you know.

It's time to realize: this is now and that was then.

It's time to take some chances and to start over again.

But you have to let go before you can finally see

The good things that will come your way…

Once you set yourself free.

Run that Race

Escape from a mind of haze and make believe.
Or soon you will find no other choice, but to leave.

Get to that straight and narrow road, the one so few seek.
And run the race without the load that has made you very weak.

Temptation may creep in and you'll think you want to use.
But you mustn't forget: you're in a race you can't afford to lose.

The reward you receive, in itself, is the best of them all.
It's knowing that the race you ran, you won

And didn't fall.

Another Piece of Cake?

My life sucks, nothing goes right.
I'm never happy… I'm always uptight.
I don't think I'm doing anything wrong.
Yet, nothing good seems to come along.

What sucks even more is being alone.
I try showing love but it's never shown.
I'm eating so much that I'm getting fat.
If I had someone…I wouldn't do that.

It really sucks that I need another car.
Mine is so old it doesn't take me far.
But I need to buy my make-up and stuff.
So how could I ever save up enough?

I hate where I live, I should move away.
Find new friends and a nicer place to stay.
Or maybe I should try a new hairstyle.
Ah, but that'll only last for a little while.

If it didn't suck, I know how I'd be:
I wouldn't let anything get to me.
I want to be happy, but what'll it take?
Oh well, I think I'll just have…

Another piece of cake!

In Other Words:

If you want love…you've got to give it.

If you want happiness…you've got to live it.

If you want wisdom…you've got to learn it.

If you want money…you've got to earn it.

If you want peace…you've got to make it.

If you want time…you've got to take it.

If you want respect…you've got to show it.

If you want truth...you've got to know it.

In other words:

If you want flowers instead of weeds…

All you've got to do is plant the seeds.

Giving Up Gets You NOWHERE

On every road of life there is something to learn.
Don't get discouraged if you take a wrong turn.
It's okay if you make a mistake now and then.
Just try not to make the same one again.

Should one become bumpy? Don't stop, go slow.
Getting over the bumps is the only way to grow.
Of if you're in a tunnel and lost for what to do:
Keep on going…you'll see light coming through.

Giving up sounds easy but it gets you nowhere.
You'll always be unsettled, going here and there.
It's best to make it down every road, my friend.
You'll be so much wiser when you get to the end.

Will You Swim, Or Sink?

Instead of planting flowers, all I expect are weeds.
Instead of making things better, I worry about my needs.
Instead of having patience, I complain things take too long.
Instead of thinking someone's right, I think they're wrong.
Instead of dealing with problems, I end up walking away.
Instead of trying to move ahead, I live for yesterday.
Instead of being happy, I find reasons to be sad.
Instead of seeing the good, I always look at the bad.
Instead of saving money, I spend it way too fast.
Instead of believing in love, I don't think it will last.

Now if this is about you: change the way you think.
It's what will determine whether you'll swim, or sink.

If You Think Your Life Sucks:

THINK HOW IT WOULD BE

If you lost your eyesight and could no longer see.
If you lost your legs and could no longer walk.
Or perhaps your voice and could no longer talk.

If you think your life sucks: think what you'd do
If a loved one was suddenly taken from you.
If your house washed away by a hurricane.
Or you had to live in a whole lot of pain.

If you think your life sucks: think what you'd say
If you met someone who had to live that way.
Do you think you'd say your life sucked then?
If so, I think…you better think again.

How a Smile Could Make a Difference

You see light in the darkest places, when you smile.
You're the winner of many races, when you smile.
You take a mood from gloom to cheer, with your smile.
Others enjoy having you near…because of your smile.
It's hard when things are going wrong, to be able to smile.
But they won't for very long…if you just try to smile.

Living in a world where so many people don't:
More smiles are needed, especially because they won't.

So consider the earth a garden and let your smile plant seeds
That will grow, just like flowers…instead of all the weeds.
And on life's journey, if you give one to someone each day:
Not only it will make a difference to them,

But it will take you a long way.

Wisdom

We have much to gain by having wisdom.

We have much to gain by wanting to learn.

However, we have more to lose

By not making it matter.

Having wisdom is like applause received

For a role well-played.

We should learn by our mistakes,

As we would a play, after many rehearsals.

Without wisdom, we get little respect.

Without rehearsals…no applause.

Because our role wasn't convincing

For an audience to take home.

PART TWO

Meeting Each Other Half Way to Find the Difference

What Marriage is All About

On a Marital Journey there are many decisions to make.
Be sure you think ahead about what each one will take.

Always walk together, however, allow each other space,
And with good communication, you will walk at the same pace.

Should Marital Problems arise: don't go your separate ways.
Stand by your vows "to stay together the rest of your days."

Vows shouldn't be broken. They are binding till death do you part.
Using them as your foundation will always give you a fresh start.

And one day you'll look back…glad you worked things out.
You see: staying together is how you learn together,

What marriage is all about.

Words to A Child

Stay close to your parents as they walk you through the years.
For one day on your own, you'll face challenges and fears.

Now is the time that they can help you understand,
Your ups, and your downs, and give you a reassuring hand.

Stay close to your parents, for the time will slip away.
One day you will appreciate what you are learning today.

Know that a parent can also be a very good friend.
Many will come and many will go,

But they will be there in the end.

Words to a Parent

Parents: listen when your child speaks, this shows he is in need
Of an open ear, and of an open mind…of a parent who will lead.

Pay attention to what he is saying. His words are important too.
Especially when he is trying to explain something to you.

This will give him the foundation to get him through those years.
To get them through those challenges, and… through those fears.

Know that a child can also become a very good friend.
When you need him the most, he too,

Will be there in the end.

Respect, Between A Parent and A Teen

I will listen to your words, but allow me to express my feelings.

I will be open to your suggestions, but allow me to make decisions.

I will abide by your rules, but allow me to take some chances.

I will never deprive you of my time, but allow me to have my own.

I will always try my hardest, but allow me my mistakes.

By allowing me these things, you have my utmost respect.

Because you allowed me that…from you.

How Long Could A Friendship Last?

What becomes of a friendship
When a friend has moved away:
Depends on how strong it was
As to how strong it will stay.

Holding all the memories
Deep within your heart:
Although you are far away
You won't feel so far apart.

What becomes of a friendship
Also depends on the time spent:
Staying in touch to show how much
The friendship has meant.

A friendship will last a lifetime.
Especially if you keep in mind:
No matter how far apart you are,
"A good friend is hard to find."

A Dog, a Best Friend?

The way you treat a dog will all depend
On whether or not he becomes your best friend.
Show him respect and he'll show it to you.
Otherwise he'll do what you don't want him to.

He'll pee on the floor… bark all day long.
Instead of doing right, he'll do what's wrong.
And if you hit him, you're the one he'll blame.
He won't even come when you call his name.

Give a dog love and he'll always be there.
He'll sit right by you in your favorite chair.
Every time you leave he'll stay by the door
Waiting to go outside instead of on the floor.

Remember, a dog has feelings like you do.
So treat him the way you'd want him to…you.
Because once he becomes your best friend:
He will be…right down to the end.

No Matter What It Takes

When you appreciate each other, there is no doubt:

Love will grow… no matter what may come about.

When you listen to each other with your heart and mind:

No matter what…understanding you will find.

And when you forgive each other for your mistakes:

You will stay together…no matter what it takes.

Coming "From the Heart"

Accept me as I am…imperfect I may be.
I come from a past that is yet in front of me.

Accept me as I am. It is within my heart
To be with you forever, or until we have to part.

And I will… you, with all that makes you, YOU.
Including your past, and… your imperfections too.

This is what it will take for our relationship to grow.
Along with honesty, kindness, and respect we must show.

It's the seeds we plant that will keep us from growing apart
If we water them daily, with love…coming "from the heart."

We Are Still Just One, of Two

I will always love you, although it may not always show.

I will always need you, although you may not always know.

I will always listen to you, although I may not always agree.

I will always give of myself, although I must keep some for me.

I will always be there for you, although at times I may be late.

I will always help you, although you may have to wait.

I will always give my heart, although I must keep it close by.

I will always trust you, although at times I may ask why.

And I will always accept the independent side of you.

Even though we are together: we are still just one, of two.

Then...We Will Know

Lost by unspoken thoughts are the lives we've been sharing.

With tension we're tied in knots, as we catch each other staring.

With dreams being shattered, and hopes disappearing:

Our minds are scattered, because of what we're not hearing.

So let's talk: to find once again you, and once again me.

Then...we will know.

She Said:

You don't show me love as you did long ago.
You're not the same person I used to know.
Whenever I want to have time with you:
You always say you got things to do.

You don't bring me gifts as you did long ago.
You're not the same person I used to know.
Every time there's something I want to say:
All you ever do is walk away.

You don't take me out as you did long ago.
You're not the same person I used to know.
I realize my nagging has been bothering you:
But what is a woman supposed to do?

He Said:

Every time I tried showing love to you:
You acted as though you didn't want me to.
And I only walk away when you start to yell.
Sometimes you make my life a living hell.

The last time I brought you a gift, you said:
"You should have gotten me flowers instead."
You're never satisfied with anything I do.
So why should I bother trying to please you?

And I don't take you out as I did long ago.
You nag me in front of everyone we know.
Now I believe the problem is really with you.
So tell me: what is a man supposed to do?

Try Some Humility

Don't let a disagreement turn into a fight.
It could end up going on day and night.
Does it really matter who's right or wrong?
Or is it more important that you get along?

If it's something simple, why not let it go.
It could blow over before you even know.
If it's something serious, talk things out.
Get to the bottom of what they're about.

But you should cool off before you do.
Things will be much easier for you.
And always listen with a humble heart.
Otherwise you may grow further apart.

Humility is more beneficial than pride.
It proves…you have nothing to hide.
Yes, it's important to communicate,
But… come to an agreement

Before it's too late!

About Those "Little Things"

We've been drifting apart more it seems,
Though my heart is filled with hopeful dreams.

As each day passes I keep wondering why
It has come down to where, we don't even try.

I remember those little things we used to do.
Setting time aside, just for me and you.

The things we would always remember to say
When a lift was needed, in some small way.

The thank you's given for a nice thing done,
Agreeing on the big things as though we were one,

Or the times we would sit and talk for awhile,
Exchanging a kiss, a touch, or a smile.

Yes, so many little things helped us to grow.
Like lighting a candle, just to watch it glow.

A hug unexpected in the middle of the day
Or a call from work, to say "I'm on my way."

What happened to those things that we don't do now?
Have we pushed them aside, to get lost somehow?

Well as I look back, I believe I can say:
"We allowed too many things… to get in our way."

For the Sake of Your Kids

DON'T FIGHT:

Did you know they take it to bed at night?
Did you know it affects the way they grow?
Here's something else I think you should know:

When they're young they look for places to hide.
They hold all the fear and tension inside.
When they're older they just try to stay gone.
They're sick of all the fighting that goes on.

Kids should be raised feeling good, not bad.
And this depends on you, Mom and Dad.
The example you set as husband and wife,
They'll remember…the rest of their life.

You should try and learn to talk things out.
Or… stop doing what it is you fight about.
Because if this behavior continues to go on,
Before you know…your kids will be gone.

And they'll have many problems, only to say:
"Look mom and dad, you made it this way."
So for everyone's sake, put the fights to rest.
Kids deserve your very, very best.

PART THREE

Coming to a Realization to Appreciate what Matters

I Lost, but I Found

I lost myself being a wife, giving all that I could give.

Working at it so hard…I forgot for myself how to live.

I lost myself through motherhood, being the best I could be.

Always putting the children first…forgetting about me.

Then I lost myself again, looking back on those days.

And realized what I lost… I had found in many ways.

It's not only the respect I get from a grateful family,

But I found I have the time now to think about me.

Those Wonderful Years You Had

Losing the one you love is hard to face.
You wake up in the morning to an empty space.
Wondering how you'll get through another day
And if the pain you're feeling will ever go away.

Things you did together that you try on your own.
Just bring back memories to do them alone.
You break down crying thinking you'd be strong.
After all, they've been in your life for so long.

The most difficult part is realizing they are gone.
You don't want to think about having to move on.
Knowing this is what they would want you to do,
You try, just to find…it's impossible to.

Yes, this is a reality that is so hard to face.
Left are only memories to fill that empty space.
But in time the memories that once made you sad,
Make you smile when you think of all…

Those wonderful years you had.

Enjoying the Grandkids

Being a grandparent is so much fun.
Even if I don't get other things done.
Even if my grandkids wear me out.
But that's okay…it's what it's all about.

I show them off everywhere I go.
Sometimes to people I don't even know.
I spoil them rotten, but that's okay too.
Isn't that what I'm supposed to do?

I always give in when I know I shouldn't.
If I try getting mad at them, I couldn't.
But that's okay, they grow up so fast.
I want to enjoy this time while it lasts.

Rebuilding the Spirit

I have lingered in many places whimpering as a child
Hiding from the world, a person...defiled.

Filled with anger, my days...draining and cold.
For being young, I was feeling very old.

The guilt I held within took away a happy soul.
Looking for places to hide became my only goal.

Remembering to pray if ever in distress,
I humbled myself with words...hard to express.

A voice spoke out: "My child, you musn't feel guilt."
Upon realizing this...my spirit was rebuilt.

I have since moved on with dignity and pride.
Instead of always looking for...places to hide.

Think How it Affects a Child

I've lived in many places… shoved around.
I've seen many faces, but never heard a sound.
I've walked miles until my shoes wore out.
I'm in the foster files as "nothing to talk about."

I'd try to find my mother if I knew where to begin.
I went to see my father, but they said he wasn't in.
Learned my brother moved away years ago.
I can't get information from anyone I know.

I often wonder why it was me they gave away.
Was it because I couldn't hear a word they'd say?
I shouldn't feel guilty, being deaf wasn't my choice.
I'd like to speak my mind, but…I also have no voice.

At times I may feel lost but I will never lose my pride.
I go through life trying to take everything in stride.
Although I can't change the past or make it disappear:
I will always be grateful for each day that I am here.

But I will never forget the times I cried feeling alone.
Missing out on all the love a child should be shown.
So please pay attention to these words I'm writing today.
"Think how it affects a child, before you give one away."

Remembering the 60's

Those were the days when it was easy to joke.
Happy times were…something to smoke.
Peace was plenty, love was in bloom…
Black lights revealed posters in your room.

Hitchhikers weren't afraid to thumb their way
Looking for a friendly place to stay.
Sharing was more; violence was rare.
The fad was wearing a flower in your hair.

To play the guitar was the thing to learn.
It wasn't always looking for money to earn.
Days went by slower. Time was taken to see
The beauty of nature, while feeling so free.

Yes, those were the days when life was fun.
No one had reason to carry a gun.
These are the days when life seems unfair.
There are few people who truly care.

Kids are lacking the attention they need.
We are living in a world with so much greed.
When I think about now and…about then:
I sure wish the 60's were back once again.

.

For Just One Day, {a Deep Regret}

To have you back for just one day, each minute would be a year.
Replacing time I threw away not appreciating you here.

My regrets would be gone by showing the love I didn't show.
My guilt would lessen, instead of growing…more than you know.

I can't go back in time, I know…the past is the past.
I just wish I could show you what I've come to realize at last.

Nothing could take the place of your being here with me.
As light keeps shining on your face…within my memory.

Along with these words, please believe me when I say:
It would be eternity to have you back…

For even just one day.

Somehow

You were always somehow able to see
The things I couldn't...in me.
And with words of advice, you'd say
What would help me along the way.

You were always somehow able to know
All the right times to show
Your comfort, and be
The one always there for me.

Yes, somehow you were able to find
A way to be not far behind.
And even though you are not here now,
I know you will always be near...

Somehow!

Now Who Could Ask for More!

Growing up was really tough.
The food we had was barely enough.
Things came from a second hand store.
And although it wasn't much,

We never asked for more.

Dad had to drive an old beat up car.
The money he made didn't go very far.
It was embarrassing to be poor.
But although we didn't have much,

We never asked for more.

At Christmastime we didn't get a lot.
We had to share everything we got.
No we didn't have much, that's for sure,
But we had so much love:

Now who could ask for more!

For You, Yourself

If you could see what I see: you would see so much beauty.

For you yourself, don't realize how beautiful you really are.

If you could feel what I feel: you would feel so much happiness.

For you yourself, don't realize just how happy you make me.

And if you were to ask me the question I know you need answered

I would say, "Yes, I truly love you"…just for you, yourself.

What Love is All About!

I wouldn't know the importance of talks filled with good advice.

I wouldn't know the pleasure of being with someone so nice.

I wouldn't know the joy of having such a wonderful day.

I wouldn't know the value of your caring in your own special way.

I wouldn't know the appreciation of a friendship, so solid, so dear.

I wouldn't know the feeling of completeness when you are here.

I wouldn't know this person I've become since I've known you.

And I wouldn't know the meaning of happiness the way I do.

But I do know how empty I would feel, without a doubt:

If I didn't know what I know now…what love is all about.

BACK IN THE DAY

A dollar took you far.

It was easy to get around without having a car.

A kid would work for a nickel or a dime.

There were no computers taking up their time.

It was safe for a child to go outside and play.

On a date…the guy would always pay.

You didn't worry if you forgot to lock your door.

Little things meant a whole lot more.

You could clearly understand the words of a song.

There was less violence, more people got along.

A good friend was always by your side.

Being gay was something to hide.

You were more relaxed instead of stressed.

You took pride in the way you dressed.

NOWADAYS

You have to watch your back.

Nobody wants to cut anybody slack.

Prices are outrageous, it's hard to live.

Homeless wear signs saying "please give."

Kids are abducted in the middle of the night.

It seems like everyone wants to fight.

It's impossible for addicts to "just say no."

Drugs are around everywhere you go.

More and more teens are bullied at school.

Another child drowned in a swimming pool.

Marriages don't last that long anymore.

The world has problems like never before.

Yes, things are worse now than back in the day,

But life doesn't have to be, unless

YOU…make it that way.

Think:

If we didn't have beautiful sunsets, the sky would be a haze.

Without sunshine, we would have cold and gloomy days.

If we didn't have color, we would see only black and white.

Without a conscience, we would do more wrong than right.

If we didn't have taste buds, everything would taste so bland.

Without oceans and rivers, we wouldn't have water at hand.

If we didn't have the rain, how would the flowers grow?

Without winters, we wouldn't know the beauty of snow.

If we didn't have the ability to hear, to feel, or to see,

We wouldn't know enjoyment: mere existence life would be.

And Just Think:

If we didn't have a wonderful Creator to provide these things,

We wouldn't know love, for this comes with all that He brings.

Now Imagine

A world without sorrow, imagine.
Peace for tomorrow, imagine.
Life without fear, unity here:
Imagine this to be true.

Love without hate, imagine.
Never being late, imagine.
Time to spare, people to care:
Imagine what this can do.

Sight for the blind, imagine.
A newness of mind, imagine.
Crime no more, no locks on a door:
Imagine these things too.

Imagine how this could change
All the sadness we see.
Now imagine this world...
A much better place to be.

Truly, a Great Accomplishment

If we can look back at life

Knowing we did our best…

We have gained wisdom.

Moving on, appreciated by many

Whose lives made a difference

Because WE, made ours matter.

This is truly a great accomplishment.

BRINGING IT ALL HOME

To Make the Difference

Walk through life leaving your worries behind.
Remember which mood could put you in a bind.

Say what you mean or don't say anything at all.
Before judging others…read the writing on the wall.

Be sure to give freely, avoid gossip in any way,
Always use tact, and take things day by day.

Live by your conscience, be the person you are.
It's okay to take a chance, but don't go too far.

Teach your children respect, every single day.
When you see a rut coming, go a different way.

Learn to be forgiving then move on and grow.
You can win that race if you're determined as you go.

Remember what it takes for a relationship to last.
Stay close to your kids…they grow up so very fast.

Come to an agreement when you talk things out.
Stay together to learn what marriage is all about.

Don't ignore your problems, or think life is unfair.
Giving up certainly won't get you anywhere.

Keep what you appreciate close to your heart.
Try to rebuild your spirit before it falls apart.

Hold on to good memories, learn by your mistakes.
Break that habit…no matter what it takes.

Think before you do something you might regret.
And always be grateful for the blessings you get.

Now if you realize what matters, the wise thing to do
Is to bring it home and make the difference.

IT IS ALL UP TO YOU!

So Long, My Friend.

Made in the USA
Middletown, DE
02 June 2022

66511261R00086